BRYAN ADAMS ANT

PIANO
VOCAL
GUITAR

ISBN 0-634-03174-0

HAL•LEONARD® CORPORATION

7777 W. BLUEMOUND RD. P.O. BOX 13819 MILWAUKEE, WI 53213

Visit Hal Leonard Online at
www.halleonard.com

PHOTOGRAPHY:
ANDREW CATLIN (BACK&FRONT)
PERRY CURTIES (INNER)
DESIGN: DIRK RUDOLPH

WWW.BRYANADAMS.COM

ALL FOR LOVE
from Walt Disney Pictures' THE THREE MUSKETEERS

Words and Music by BRYAN ADAMS,
ROBERT JOHN ™MUTT LANGE and MICHAEL KAMEN

When it's love you give ____ (I'll be a man of good
____ (I swear I'll al - ways be
____ (I'll be the fire in your

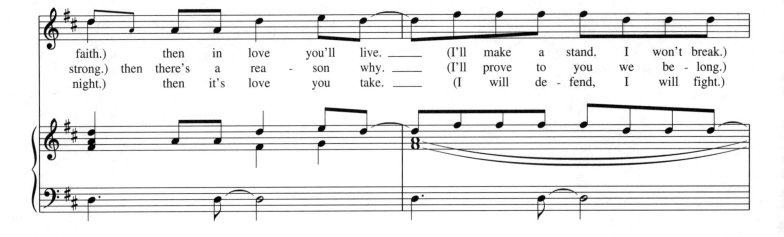

faith.) then in love you'll live. ____ (I'll make a stand. I won't break.)
strong.) then there's a rea - son why. ____ (I'll prove to you we be - long.)
night.) then it's love you take. ____ (I will de - fend, I will fight.)

I'll be the rock you can build on, ____
I'll be the wall that pro - tects you ____
I'll be there when you need me. ____

BACK TO YOU

Words and Music by BRYAN ADAMS
and ELIOT KENNEDY

Lively Rock

I've been down, I've been beat, but you did not show_

I've been so tired it; you've been in pain I could not speak. but I did not know_ it. I've been so lost You let me do

THE BEST OF ME

Words and Music by BRYAN ADAMS
and ROBERT JOHN LANGE

CAN'T STOP THIS THING WE STARTED

Words and Music by BRYAN ADAMS
and ROBERT JOHN LANGE

bro - ken - heart - ed.   I can't stop it.   I can't stop it.

I can't stop this thing we start - ed. ___   You got-ta know ___

___ it's right. ___   I can't stop this course we've plot - ted, ___

Repeat and Fade

yeah. ___

CLOUD NUMBER NINE

Words and Music by BRYAN ADAMS,
GRETCHEN PETERS and MAX MARTIN

With a steady beat

Clue num - ber one ____ was when you knocked on my door. ____
he hurt you ____ and you hurt me, ____ and

Clue num - ber two ____ was ____ the look that you wore, ____ and
that was - n't the way it was sup - posed to be. ____ So

Yeah, we won't_ come down_ to - night. _____ No, we won't_

_____ come down_ to - night, _____ 'cause the moon_

CODA

D

_____ num - ber nine. _____

A

Yeah, we can watch_ the world_ go by _____ up on cloud_

D

_____ num - ber nine. _____

G   A   D

DO I HAVE TO SAY THE WORDS?

Words and Music by BRYAN ADAMS,
JIM VALLANCE and ROBERT JOHN LANGE

CUTS LIKE A KNIFE

Words and Music by BRYAN ADAMS
and JIM VALLANCE

DON'T GIVE UP

Words and Music by BRYAN ADAMS, RAY HEDGES,
NICK BRACEGIRDLE and MARTIN BRANNIGAN

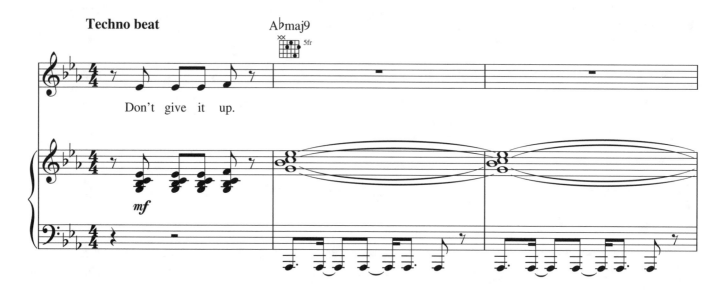

Don't give it up.

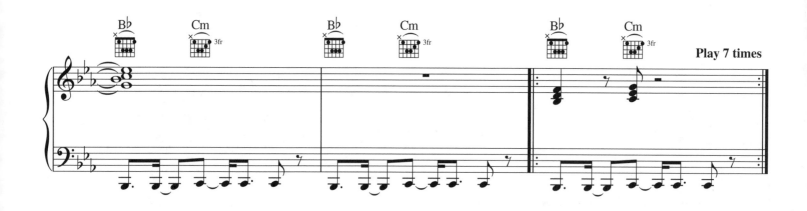

Play 7 times

Don't wor-ry if the sun don't shine. ___ You've seen it be-fore. ___

give it up.

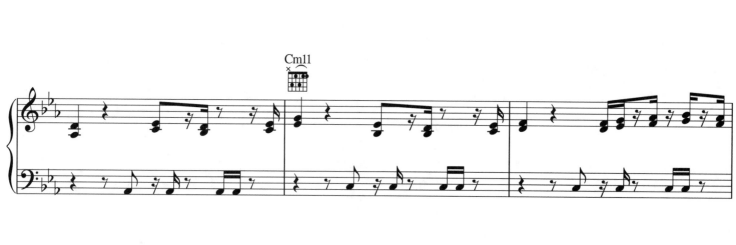

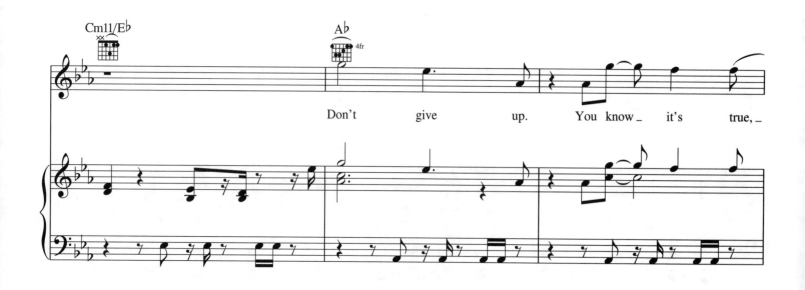

Don't give up. You know it's true,

Don't give it up.

Don't give up. You know _ it's true, _

(Everything I Do)
I DO IT FOR YOU

from the Motion Picture ROBIN HOOD: PRINCE OF THIEVES

Words and Music by BRYAN ADAMS,
ROBERT JOHN LANGE and MICHAEL KAMEN

HAVE YOU EVER REALLY LOVED A WOMAN?

from the Motion Picture DON JUAN DeMARCO

Words and Music by BRYAN ADAMS,
MICHAEL KAMEN and ROBERT JOHN LANGE

Additional Lyrics

2. To really love a woman, let her hold you
   Till ya know how she needs to be touched.
   You've gotta breathe her, really taste her.
   Till you can feel her in your blood.
   N' when you can see your unborn children in her eyes.
   Ya know ya really love a woman.

   When you love a woman
   You tell her that she's really wanted.
   When you love a woman
   You tell her that she's the one.
   Cuz she needs somebody to tell her
   That you'll always be together
   So tell me have you ever really,
   Really really ever loved a woman.

3. *Instrumental*

   Then when you find yourself
   Lyin' helpless in her arms.
   You know you really love a woman.

   When you love a woman *etc.*

HEARTS ON FIRE

Words and Music by BRYAN ADAMS
and JIM VALLANCE

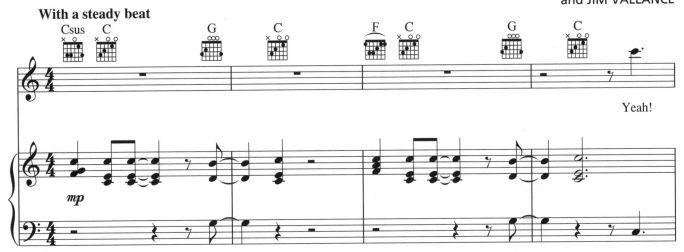

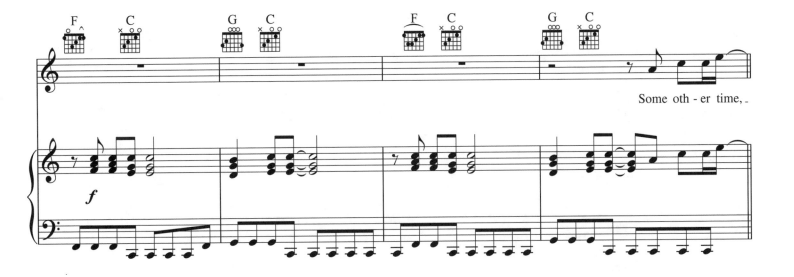

Original key: B major. This edition has been transposed up one half-step to be more playable.

HEAT OF THE NIGHT

Words and Music by BRYAN ADAMS
and JIM VALLANCE

I was caught in the cross - fire of a si - lent scream, __
Met a man with a mes - sage from the oth - er side. __
Had to pay the pip - er to call the tune. __

I FINALLY FOUND SOMEONE

from THE MIRROR HAS TWO FACES

Words and Music by BARBRA STREISAND, MARVIN HAMLISCH,
R.J. LANGE and BRYAN ADAMS

HEAVEN

Words and Music by BRYAN ADAMS
and JIM VALLANCE

I'M READY

Words and Music by BRYAN ADAMS
and JIM VALLANCE

IT'S ONLY LOVE

Words and Music by BRYAN ADAMS
and JIM VALLANCE

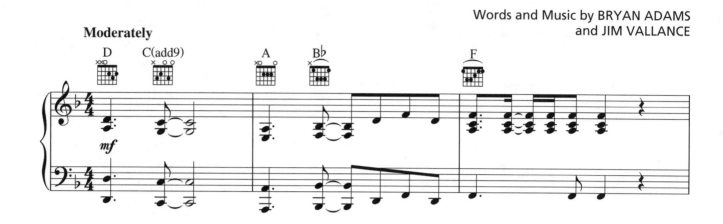

When the feel-in' is end-ed, there ain't
heart has been bro-ken, hard ___
shat - tered, ___ ain't ___

no use pre-tend-in'. Don't ya wor-ry, Well, it's on-ly love. When your
words have been spo-ken, it ain't eas-y, but it's on-ly love. And if your
noth-in' else mat-ters. It ain't o - ver, it's ___ on-ly love. If your

KIDS WANNA ROCK

Words and Music by BRYAN ADAMS
and JIM VALLANCE

Driving Rock

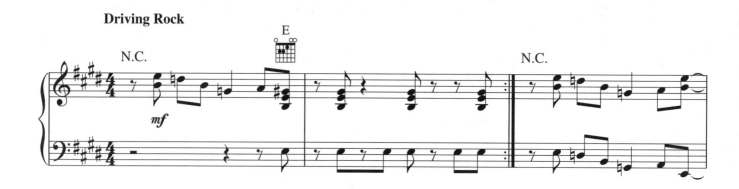

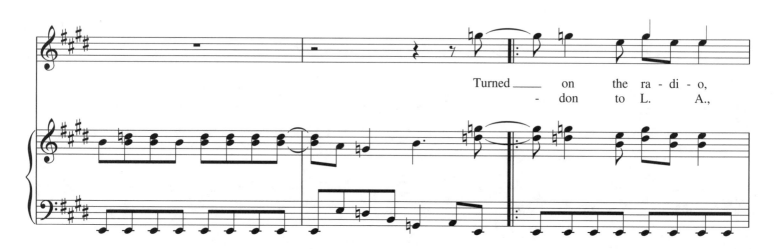

Turned ___ on the ra - di - o,
- don to L. A.,

turn it up! Yeah! Whoa!

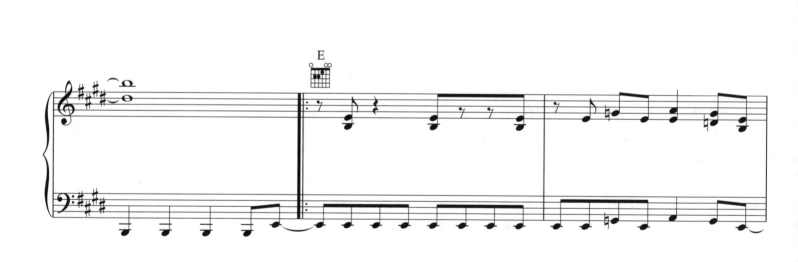

ONE NIGHT LOVE AFFAIR

Words and Music by BRYAN ADAMS
and JIM VALLANCE

LET'S MAKE A NIGHT TO REMEMBER

Words and Music by BRYAN ADAMS
and ROBERT JOHN LANGE

1. I love the way ya look to - night,__

2. (See additional lyrics)

with your hair hang-in' down on your shoul - ders.__

(ad lib. vocal)

Play 5 times for fade

Additional Lyrics

2. I love the way ya move tonight.
   Beads of sweat drippin' down your skin.
   Me lying here n' you lyin' there.
   Our shadows on the wall and our hands everywhere.

   Let's make out, let's do something amazing.
   Let's do something that's all the way.
   'Cuz I've never touched somebody
   Like the way I touch your body.
   Now I never want to let your body go.

   Let's make a night to remember, *etc.*

The Only Thing That Looks Good On Me Is You

Words and Music by BRYAN ADAMS
and ROBERT JOHN LANGE

The on-ly thing I want, ___ the on-ly thing I need, ___

___ the on-ly thing I choose, ___ the

on-ly thing ___ that looks good on me ___ is you. ___

___ I'm not

PLEASE FORGIVE ME

Words and Music by BRYAN ADAMS
and ROBERT JOHN LANGE

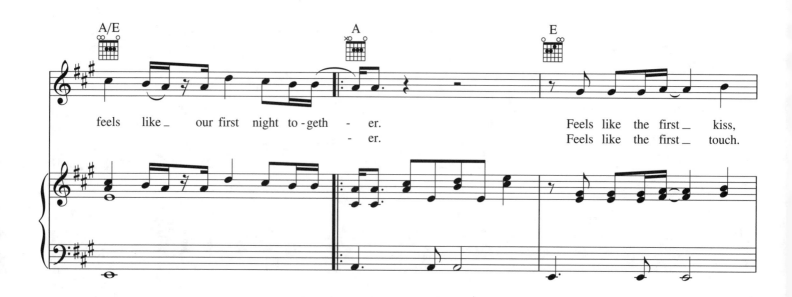

lieve me, _____ ev - 'ry word I say is true. Please for -

give me. ____ I can't stop lov - in' you.

It still

feels like _ our best times _ are to - geth-   give me. ____ I can't stop lov - in' you. _

RUN TO YOU

Words and Music by BRYAN ADAMS
and JIM VALLANCE

She says her / She's got a

love for me ___ could nev-er die. / heart of gold, ___ she'd nev-er let me down.

But that-'d change if she ev-er found out a-bout you and I. / But you're the one that al-ways turns me on and keeps me com-in' round.

Oh, __ when the feel - in's right __ I'm gon - na run all night, __ I'm gon - na

run to you. _____

SOMEBODY

Words and Music by BRYAN ADAMS
and JIM VALLANCE

I been look - in' for some -
Now who can you turn ___
When you're out on the front ___
I thought I saw the Ma -

STRAIGHT FROM THE HEART

Words and Music by BRYAN ADAMS
and ERIC KAGNA

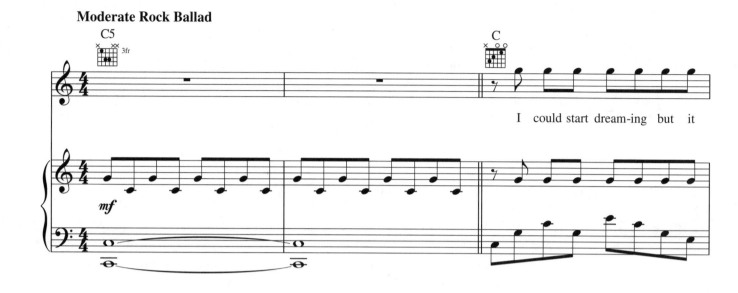

SUMMER OF '69

Words and Music by BRYAN ADAMS
and JIM VALLANCE

Moderately bright

I got my

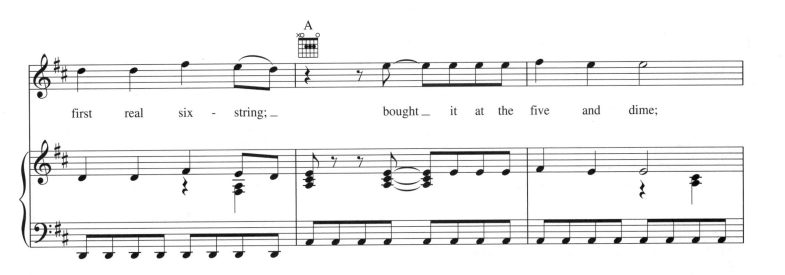

first real six - string; __ bought __ it at the five and dime; __

played __ it 'til my fin - gers __ bled; was the sum - mer of

THERE WILL NEVER BE ANOTHER TONIGHT

Words and Music by BRYAN ADAMS, JIM VALLANCE
and ROBERT JOHN LANGE

THIS TIME

Words and Music by BRYAN ADAMS
and JIM VALLANCE

THOUGHT I'D DIED AND GONE TO HEAVEN

Words and Music by BRYAN ADAMS
and ROBERT JOHN LANGE

Moderately, with a steady beat

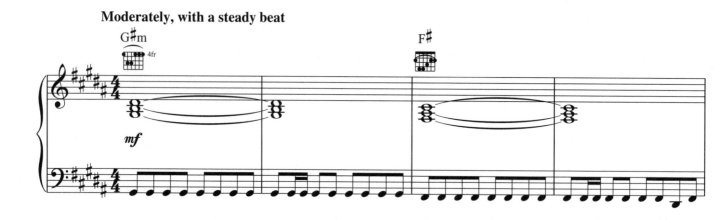

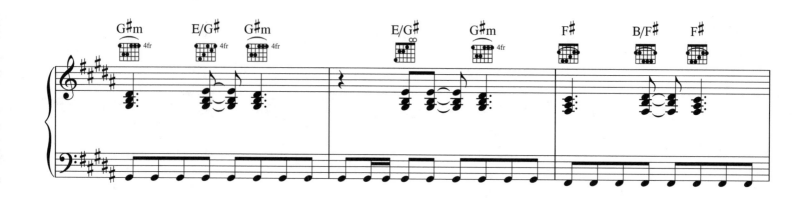

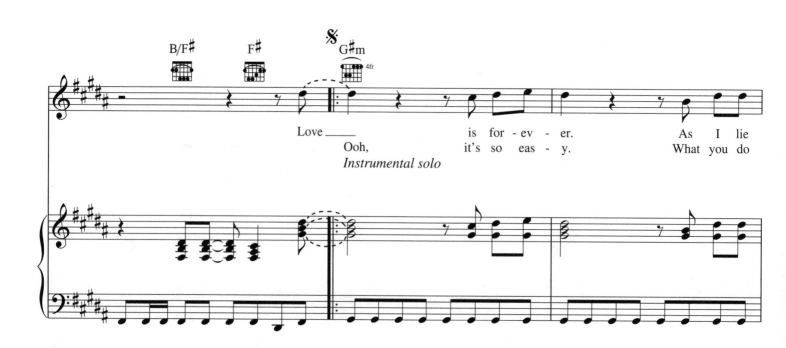

Love _____ is for - ev - er.   As I lie
Ooh,   it's so eas - y.   What you do
Instrumental solo

WHEN YOU LOVE SOMEONE

from HOPE FLOATS

Words and Music by BRYAN ADAMS,
MICHAEL KAMEN and GRETCHEN PETERS

WHEN YOU'RE GONE

Words and Music by BRYAN ADAMS
and ELIOT KENNEDY

I've been wan - d'rin' a - round __ the __ house __ all __ night, __ won - try'n' - in' up __ and __ down __ these __ streets, __

- d'rin' what __ the hell to do. __ Yeah, I'm try'n' __ to con - cen - trate, but all __ to find __ some - where to go. __ Yeah, I'm look - in' for a fa - mil - iar

__ I can think __ of is you. ____ Well, the phone __ face, but there's no __ one I know. ____ Oh, __ this __

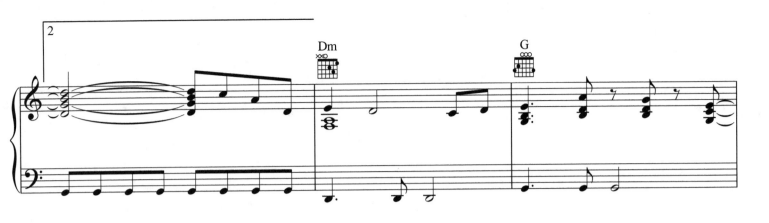